LOVE-JACKED!

DIVORCE YOUR SPOUSE, NOT YOUR DOLLARS

By

BONNIE A. SEWELL, CFP®, CDFA™, AIF®

Principal, American Capital Planning, LLC
www.wedlock-divorce.com

Disclaimer: All written content in this book is for information purposes only. Opinions expressed herein are solely those of American Capital Planning, LLC, ("ACP"). Material presented is believed to be from reliable sources and we make no representations as to its accuracy or completeness. All information and ideas should be discussed in detail with your individual advisor prior to implementation. ACPC is a registered investment advisory firm in the state of Virginia. The author and publisher are not providing legal, accounting or specific advice concerning your situation. Nothing in this book should be directly or indirectly construed or interpreted as a solicitation to sell or offer to sell investment advisory services to any residents of any state other than the state of Virginia. (Registered Investment Advisors are legally empowered to provide investment advisory services only to residents of the states in which they are licensed.)

To all children of divorce but in particular, my beloved sons
Sean and Kevin, and my beloved niece, Heather.

TABLE OF CONTENTS

INTRODUCTION

This Child of Divorce and My Grown-Up Divorce

My family has a tradition of divorce. My mom, Carol Ashby came from a "broken home", as divorce was called back then. While she lost a father in that transition, she and her four siblings were raised by two strong women, her mother Eva Grace Kavana, and a wonderful domestic woman, named Annie Johnson.

My dad left our home when I was nine. He was a decorated WWII Navy veteran and part of the Scouts and Raiders (the precursor to today's SEALs). My parents were nine years apart in age and a universe apart in most other ways.

Neighbors also said we were from a "broken home". We were certainly broke but never broken.

My mom raised my two siblings and me by sheer force and creativity. She started back to work as a secretary, quickly realized it would not pay the bills, switched to waitressing at a

Sheraton hotel in Oakbrook, Illinois and worked her way up to Catering Director. After we were grown and independent, she moved to North Carolina to start her own business. Although mindful of her health in many ways, she smoked cigarettes since her teens and sadly, died of a massive stroke at age fifty-seven.

My dad moved about four hours away for work and he would drop in and out of my life for the rest of my life. I saw where he lived twice before he died at the age of seventy-seven.

For any dad of a daughter reading this, I hope you'll make the strongest effort possible to teach your daughter what you think she should know of the world and confirm that she knows you love her. It may save decades of uncertainty for her. Further, if she learns about men from you, the man she trusts the most, she may choose well when and if she decides to marry. Otherwise, not knowing what a good man is and how he acts, speaks, follows through, loves, and shares, she may take the first offer she gets, even if it's a lousy offer. She will not know what she should wait for or expect.

I was certainly one of those girls. I picked the wrong partner and knew it fairly early on. It's difficult to admit I stayed far too long in a marriage that had died many years before it formally ended.

The trigger for me finally taking responsibility for my part and ending the marriage was my life-long friend's illness. Karen Hvorka (nee Miller) and I were friends from Kindergarten. We were two in a group of five girls that stayed friends from our childhoods through raising our own children. Karen was taller, smarter, and as the years went along, much more beautiful than me. She had an easy, rolling laugh that started low and deep in her throat. I can still call it up in my mind without her being in front of me.

Karen first started having some trouble with her leg and it took months to get a correct diagnosis. When it came, Amyotrophic lateral sclerosis-ALS or Lou Gehrig's disease, we joined Karen on an eighteen month roller coaster ride that would change all our lives and take hers.

It was my wake up call. My husband and I met my senior year in college and were married for twenty-five years. Those years were filled with corporate moves where just about the time we'd get comfortable, it was time to pull up stakes again. We never lived anywhere more than five years and some stints were just eighteen months. It was quite difficult to establish my own career and company but I did it in nearly every location and my clients have thankfully adjusted to my changing office locations without interruption to my work with them.

The marriage was always off in some way and around 1995, it began to formally die.

We were no longer intimate on any level. Time just passed. While a very pretty picture on the outside with multiple homes, nice cars, and private schools, it was very lonely on the inside.

In July 2006, I asked for a divorce. It was granted on February 22, 2007 at around 9 a.m. Due to the many moves, my income was lower than it could have been. I asked for and received temporary spousal support. My company was earning money and I continued to build it until the spring of 2008 when I merged it with a larger firm in Miami where the owners were retiring. I loved Miami and it truly felt like a new beginning.

The owners and I did part ways in the summer of 2009 and I started over once again in a new city taking my clients and opening my new firm in Northern Virginia where I live today.

It's my intention to change the world of marital and divorce financial planning with this book and with the work we do with clients. It will take couples rejecting traditional position bargaining and accepting understanding the nature and characteristics of what they've built together. They will then need to look at the worth of the marital estate and start negotiating from a place of knowledge and understanding of exactly what's at stake.

Divorce is not exclusively a woman's or man's transition, it's a family's transition. To help families preserve the assets that they alone built, we have developed the A.G.R.E.E.™ negotiating process to get to a fair and equitable settlement. Read on to understand a new way of getting safely through the transition of divorce. Your future financial freedom depends on it.

THE GAME OF DIVORCE

*Why "winning"
isn't everything*

The nature of games includes players, strategies and movement towards a goal in the context of the payoff or cost of any particular move or strategy. Divorcing your spouse should not be thought of as a game. That is destructive to you, your spouse, your children, and your assets. If you can think of the divorce industry as a game, however, you will begin to understand what you've just signed up for in order to complete your divorce.

A study of divorce by the New York law firm Mishcon de Reya found that 50 percent of children believe that their parents put their own interests over their children's following separation. Further, in half of the cases, parents admitted they dragged their heels, making the legal process even longer. Some of these people admitted that the motivation was to make the process more painful for their ex-spouse. This is an example of spouse game playing with divorce. This is strongly discouraged.

Knowing you are dealing with a game player makes it very difficult to proceed with either mediation or collaborative process or in any way if the other person is bound and determined to be unreasonable. It may sound a little crass, but if you think about the divorce process as a kind of game and you devise a strategy to play the game fairly, yet well, you may actually help yourself rather than to believe it is a process in which you have very little control.

Certainly when real humans are involved who have once cared enough about each other to get married and no longer care enough about each other to stay married, we need to consider that treating divorce like a game also has the risk of trivializing a very difficult transition for everyone. But keeping in mind that divorce and the process of divorce have game-like qualities will help you when you put yourself in the place to decide which way you would like to divorce.

1. The cruelest divorce myth is that getting "your day in court" is good. Make no mistake; the divorce process today benefits the attorneys far more than their clients.

2. The next most cruel divorce myth is that you'll come out of it with your former lifestyle intact.

> In my experience, without fair negotiation, you won't have anything resembling your former lifestyle after being financially shredded in the current family law system.

In a litigated divorce, people often fantasize about their day in court—the reality is that the family law courts do not enjoy the time or money to consider your case the way you've imagined it. They're not going to meet your children, and they have heard it all when it comes to how badly you've been treated by your spouse. You are giving power you have to decide your financial and parenting future over to a third party stranger, and you will be forced to abide by those decisions.

Good divorce planning doesn't favor one spouse over the other. Poor divorce planning uses the detraction technique in the same immature way we've set up politics—my team vs. your team—instead of seeking good solutions for all. When we make divorcing specifically about women or men, we distract ourselves from *taking care of the family*.

I want to be exceedingly clear here. *Do not* treat each other (you and your spouse) as if this is a game, but *do* treat the divorce industry as if it is a game. Figure out what's best for you and your spouse to win it so that you both have a place to rebuild from. In the end, the divorce industry (like our medical, judicial, and other big industries) will swirl you in, take your money, and spit you out the other side where you get to live with the results. Then it will move on to the next two players.

So, let's take a look at each kind of divorce and their game qualities. We'll try to think of them in terms of strategy with the aim of getting through the process leaving people financially whole to go forward with their lives. We'll explore the ways you can divorce and we will try to be as jargon free as possible. Since we are still dealing essentially with the breaking of a contract, some jargon is necessary.

Uncontested (Pro Se) divorce

Uncontested (Pro Se) divorce means you are divorcing without the representation of an attorney. You still have to fill out certain legal forms to divorce this way, and it can be appropriate for those who cannot afford to hire any experts and for those marriages without children or assets. Some people end up choosing this after becoming frustrated with the attorneys they've hired and paid.

In terms of game playing, there is the least amount of exposure to the family law system in this version of divorce, and so it's pretty simple; either you and your spouse will work things out between you or you won't.

Whoever files in the uncontested divorce is referred to as the Petitioner, and the other spouse is called the Respondent. Things to consider include where (i.e., what county) to file, how to file (all necessary paperwork in your state), and how and when to notify your spouse of your filing.

Some states have residency requirements before you can file. Once you know this and you qualify, you can get the forms needed from the county clerk. Nearly everything in divorce involves a fee, and that's true here too. There will be filing fees, and if you cannot afford them, you can file an affidavit (simply a document stating that you are telling the truth about whatever it is you are claiming; in this case, that you cannot afford the fee).

After you file, you need to notify your spouse in the required method of your court clerk's office. Usually, one of the following ways suffices: 1) serve them yourself, and have them sign a waiver acknowledging they've been served, 2) hire a process server to do this for you, or 3) request that your spouse be served through a public posting if you do not know their location.

Even though this process can be the simplest in terms of time and paperwork, you may still need to have temporary orders to cover the time period between filing and final divorce. If you have been unable to work out a temporary agreement with your spouse that covers custody, child support, spousal support, who pays what bills, etc., you can each hire an attorney to work towards a temporary agreement and if that fails, the attorneys can set up a pre-trial hearing. Temporary orders allow you to continue functioning financially and as parents as you move through the process. In addition to the items mentioned above, these temporary agreements include who stays in the marital home and what cash and assets are available during this period. As I just described it, you can see how the cost will escalate as you move from doing it yourselves to going to court. The court system removes decision making from you and gives it to the court.

Sometimes, court is the best solution. An example of this is when one party needs immediate financial support and the other party is unwilling to come to an agreement.

Be certain that the agreements are indeed temporary. When you better understand the characteristics of your assets and parenting challenges, you can move towards a final settlement agreement.

Eventually you will file a notice for the final divorce hearing. Every state has their own laws, and if yours has a waiting period, you'll need to meet this before the final date can be set. When the date is set, you have to notify your spouse.

Both spouses should gather financial information, and any related documents should be shared. What *all* divorces are working toward is a marital settlement agreement (MSA), also called a property settlement agreement (PSA), depending on that particular state.

Let's take a look at this critical document. This settlement agreement dictates what will be split, how much each party gets, when they get it, how they get it, arrangements for child support, spousal support, custody, and visitation. This is one of the divorce documents that must be written well in order for you to have the desired and agreed upon outcome.

Uncontested divorces even with agreeable parties can run into emotional or financial issues that frustrate one or both people. Sometimes letting an issue rest can make it less threatening. A typical emotional issue is the introduction of a new person in the life of one of the spouses. Acknowledging that the divorce is going forward anyway and that no marital assets will be spent on the new person can keep the discussions moving. A financial issue that typically comes up is credit card spending. It's important to agree early to spending limits that do not increase debt or threaten the trust needed to complete a settlement agreement.

During our first consultation, very often women tell me that their spouse is being very agreeable. This, of course, is to be encouraged. In my experience providing financial planning advice, it's also a little unrealistic to expect this pleasantness throughout and after the actual divorce. Most of the time, when it comes to splitting up money and property, even the most even-handed people become unglued to some degree. This is the nature of splitting up what in some cases has taken decades to build. It is normal to feel freaked out. It is normal to feel like things are being taken from you (both spouses often feel this), and it is normal to need lots of information to understand how the split works today and down the road.

If you get to this part of the process in an uncontested divorce and you get stuck here, it would be good to consider other options. I have seen couples develop a kind of decision paralysis and stay at this impasse for *years*. I don't recommend it. The options available to you if you cannot move forward could include seeking counseling or involve hiring legal assistance.

The final caution on an uncontested divorce is when one of the parties has a poor or incomplete understanding of the assets and income at stake. It would be the rare couple who would not benefit from meeting with a Certified Divorce Financial Analyst to increase or confirm understanding of the worth of the marital estate to be split and the tax ramifications of any particular split.

Mediation

If the two of you cannot come to an agreement on your own, the next option most people turn to is mediation. Many proponents of mediation suggest this as a nonadversarial way to divorce. It certainly can be, but I've seen it used inappropriately too often between spouses who have no intention of mediating anything. They are bound and determined to be adversarial, and so mediation just becomes another expensive step in the divorce process and with an unsatisfactory outcome.

It can work but, in my experience, only with reasonable parties participating. I've been in mediations where all parties sat through six hours of mediation. Mediators sometimes tout success rates or wins. This means that if at the end of the day (or days) they can get both parties to sign a piece of paper, they have then settled. Even if the signed outcome simply says they'll move the next meeting out six months, for that day, they've "settled." I have seen retired judges in this capacity who are, frankly, just awful in their roles.

In 2001, the American Bar Association developed thirteen model standards for use in mediation. If you choose this method, please take the time to become familiar with them so that you get what you pay for.

The standard I have seen most often violated is Standard IV:

A family mediator shall conduct the mediation process in an impartial manner. A family mediator shall disclose all actual and potential grounds of bias and conflicts of interest reasonably known to the mediator. The participants shall be free to retain the mediator by an informed, written waiver of the conflict of interest. However, if a bias or conflict of interest clearly impairs a mediator's impartiality, the mediator shall withdraw regardless of the express agreement of the participants.

1. Impartiality means freedom from favoritism or bias in word, action or appearance, and includes a commitment to assist all participants as opposed to any one individual.

2. Conflict of interest means any relationship between the mediator, any participant or the subject matter of the dispute, that compromises or appears to compromise the mediator=s impartiality.

3. A family mediator should not accept a dispute for mediation if the family mediator cannot be impartial.

4. A family mediator should identify and disclose potential grounds of bias or conflict of interest upon which a mediator's impartiality might reasonably be questioned. Such disclosure should be made prior to the start of mediation and in time to allow the participants to select an alternate mediator.

5. A family mediator should resolve all doubts in favor of disclosure. All disclosures should be made as soon as practical after the mediator becomes aware of the bias or potential conflict of interest. The duty to disclose is a continuing duty.

6. A family mediator should guard against bias or partiality based on the participants = personal characteristics, background or performance at the mediation.

7. A family mediator should avoid conflicts of interest in recommending the services of other professionals.
8. A family mediator shall not use information about participants obtained in mediation for personal gain or advantage
9. A family mediator should withdraw pursuant to Standard IX if the mediator believes the mediator's impartiality has been compromised or a conflict of interest has been identified and has not been waived by the participants.

It can be quite a hurdle to object to bias if you're already in the meditation process and trying to avoid the courtroom. Here's something else a lot of people don't think through: the players include the two attorneys, the mediator, a financial professional, and a recorder.

Again, it's important to consider the relationship of you and your spouse. If you are not able to reasonably talk and negotiate with each other, mediation is not going to work. It is dependent on two reasonable people. The biggest frustration here is when I see attorneys recommend mediation to two people who simply cannot communicate on any level without emotion. No mediator I've seen can overcome that relationship. And the attorneys are padding their own bills when they suggest it for an embattled couple.

Here's how one of these mediations went for a client of mine who was trying to modify spousal support. This modification was a clause written into the final settlement, which is the only reason it was available as an option.

Neither spouse was happy with the other to the point where they never spoke outside an attorney's office. They were stuck on the issue of spousal support, and both sides wanted dramatic changes; one wanted a large increase, the other a large decrease. Mediation was suggested and scheduled. Before mediation, the retired judge (mediator) asked for a narrative from both attorneys. I do not believe he read them, since everything discussed in mediation seemed to surprise him. As the hours dragged on with no movement, he seemed to be exhibiting bias in the form of repeating allegations from one side in what was ultimately a no-fault divorce many years earlier. Re-living the issues leading to the divorce had no place in a modification mediation related to a no-fault divorce. It wasted time, served as a distraction, and ultimately produced nothing of value, except a nice payday for the professional players in the room.

In mediation, six hours is a full day. At the end of this day, neither party moved in true negotiation. And so all that was accomplished was that both parties agreed to meet again in six months. By the way, the mediator and both attorneys put a "win" in their columns because they got the parties to sign something. I can tell you my client did not feel like a winner. My client felt snookered by a process that was incorrectly suggested for two parties who cannot communicate on any level.

That little negotiation cost $300/hour for the mediator, $250/hour for me (the financial professional), $550/hour for each side's attorney, and a $75/hour for the recorder (court reporter hired for the day but unused since there was no movement or change in the settlement to record for the court) for a total of $10,350 for the six-hour day. Not to mention lost work time for my client. There are more mediation bills coming for this couple and, I suspect, ultimately a day in court. To avoid this, get agreement with your attorney that the process will not go six hours if significant movement can't be made in the first few hours.

And there are simply some times when a person unrealistically wants to punish the other side by insisting on court. The person insisting on getting their "day in court" does not realize that is the place of least control. But if you're dealing with an unreasonable party, it may be the only way to end it.

But before we go to that extreme, let's look at another alternative: collaborative divorce. If you believe you want to participate in the collaborative law divorce process, you need to know it is not as simple or as inexpensive as often portrayed. Anyone who has worked in divorce learns very quickly that the alternative dispute resolution choices leave a lot to be desired.

In the collaborative law game, the idea is that you and your spouse each hire attorneys who are specifically trained to work cooperatively. They disclose everything for fair negotiations and meet with each other and discuss the settlement. So as with all games, you need to understand the board or space you're playing in, the players, and the rules. The space is generally a nice conference room or office. The original version of this game only included attorneys and their clients. In today's version of the collaborative game, it includes an entire team of professionals.

To their credit, this appears to be the only place attorneys have admitted they can't and shouldn't be the only client representatives. Today's collaborative process addresses the legal, financial, emotional, and parenting aspects of divorce.

Here are the rules:

Legal:

Each of you hire your own attorney trained in the collaborative process. These attorneys are to advise you of the laws applicable to your circumstances. You have the authority to decide which legal rights and responsibilities will be relied on in your case.

Financial:

Each of you hire your own financial professional. Part of the collaborative process is to agree to transparency and an open exchange of financial information. The financial professional gathers all relevant data and produces financial reports as well as potential scenarios of the splitting of property.

Emotional:

Each of you hires a mental health professional (MHP). The MHP is a resource for the team and is charged with assisting both parties in dealing with each other through negotiation after consideration of their history together. Unlike a therapist, their discussions do not enjoy the same confidentiality as in therapy.

Parenting:

Together, you hire a child specialist. This person helps the parents formulate co-parenting plans, time-sharing agreements, and other matters where children are involved.

Why does a process that appears to address most needs still often fail? In part, because it is still a form of position bargaining. Each of your positions is advocated by your attorneys. The process can go on for many months, and the expense can rival a court case. After all, you are paying for up to *seven* professional team members!

Let's take a look at the financial professional in the collaborative process. In most divorces, financial aspects are front and center and can even be the motivation to seek divorce. Remember, in real divorce (not the mythological one where everyone comes out okay or the other popular version where you punish your spouse), both of you are dividing what will be fewer resources, more modest lifestyles, and potential financial scarcity for several years post divorce.

The financial pro brings accurate and current information to the table about the resources and tax impact on the family. They are your reality check. They not only look at today but look many years out to determine if the settlement scenarios are equitable.

In this game, the financial person often shows up as a "neutral." That means they do not advocate a particular position and instead simply indicate the financial outcomes of any particular settlement offer. I find the use of the word *neutral* particularly interesting here, and I agree that it's best to avoid position bargaining. It feels naïve however, to indicate that a negotiated outcome may be heard, seen, or felt as "neutral." Instead, I prefer language that indicates what is actually happening—a negotiation that may be uneven due to the resources available but will not be unfair.

At the beginning of this game, you would have signed an agreement that lays out the participation process, including that both parties agree not to litigate. The attorneys also would have signed this participation agreement. If any party violates the agreement, the professional team withdraws from the process, and you both get to start over with new counsel.

The other hallmark of a functioning collaborative agreement process is that it is open, transparent, and complete. While there are no do-overs in divorce, if the parties participate fraudulently, any agreement can later be set aside.

How can the collaborative process be gamed by the professional players? The usual suspects are the attorneys, as they have the most to gain (lots more fees) from a protracted process. When they have leverage such as both of your having to start over if someone decides to litigate, it ripens the potential for abuse by the paid players. That leverage should be used to keep you both negotiating in good faith. Your leverage is to do so and reduce the time in negotiation.

Since an attorney's livelihood depends on constantly "eating what they kill," some previously litigious attorneys have climbed in the collaborative bed, so to speak, in order to pull fees in from the latest divorce industry trend. Make sure the collaborative attorney you hire lives and breathes good faith negotiation skills.

Finally, since the strength of negotiation in the collaborative process is entirely dependent on the strength of the players, you cannot be certain of the strengths (or lack of them) until you're already in the very expensive process. Attorneys are rated, **www. martindale.com** but it can be a true challenge to accurately guage their expertise as it applies to your needs.

Now for a research-based reality check from the International Academy of Collaborative Professionals (IACP): in the Spring 2012 issue of *The Collaborative Review*, they reported on 930 cases from 2006 through 2010. Nearly all professionals had collaborative training. The survey participants included 59 percent of all husbands and 59 percent of all wives, all between forty and fifty-four years old. Fifty three percent of husbands earned one hundred thousand dollars or more, and only 16 percent of husbands earned less than fifty thousand dollars. Only 13 percent of wives earned one hundred thousand dollars or more, and 62 percent of wives earned less than fifty thousand dollars. The value of the assets in these cases usually exceeded two hundred thousand dollars with a significant majority worth more than five hundred thousand dollars. Children were involved in 84 percent of these cases. From these numbers, we can conclude there is a lot at stake for the families involved.

When people contemplate divorce, everyone wants to know how long it will take. In the cases studied, *less than 14 percent concluded in three months or less*. About 13 percent finished in three to four months, with 18 percent finishing in five to six months. Another 14 percent finished between seven to eight months, and 21 percent finished in nine to twelve months. Another 18 percent finished between thirteen to twenty-four months, with 3 percent taking more than two years to complete.

The next question from most people is, how much will it cost? There are two ways to look at this in the collaborative model: the attorneys' fees or the team's fees. Based on the IACP's study, if we look at the team, the average fees paid to both attorneys was $20,884. The average fees paid to the mental health professional was $3,858, and the average fees paid to the financial professional was $4,421. Total average fees paid to all professionals was $24,185.

For that money, you can expect to have up to four face-to-face meetings between attorneys and clients in 63 percent of cases, three meetings with attorneys, clients, and mental health professionals in 11 percent of cases, and two meetings with lawyers, clients, and financial professionals in 18 percent of cases.

Twenty-one percent of cases reported having five or more meetings with their collaborative teams. These meetings lasted an average of 2.5 hours.

When we look at the cost of fees paid by model, we see the average total fees paid in team cases was $34,071. Of course, cost is affected by region.

What is not clear from the study is how both parties were holding up financially. In the cases from 2006, four years out may be enough time to see if the settlement was actually fair and equitable. In the cases closer to the end of study, the participants are not likely to know for a few more years.

These cases were rated for difficulty, and as the level of difficulty increased, so did the involvement of the financial specialist. Sixty percent of the cases that involved incomes over two hundred thousand dollars included the financial specialist; 57 percent of the estates over one million dollars included the financial specialist. This makes sense as very few attorneys are trained in personal or business finance. Remember, in divorce, we're only negotiating money and parenting issues.

In 90 percent of cases involving a financial specialist, they typically held a CFP, CDFA, or CPA credential. Average hourly rates ranged from $150 to $300/hour, and they spent twenty-five to thirty hours per case for an average fee of $4,500 to $9,000.

The collaborative process works best when you have trained professionals, reasonable clients, and good intentions from all parties. If any one of these pieces is in short supply, you may spend a significant amount of money only to have to start over when it becomes clear collaborative divorce is not an option for you.

The Worst Divorce Choice—I'll see you in court

You're in the 5 to 15 percent that just could not work it out any other way. Well, yes, you may see them in court, but it will cost you. And because family law courts are so overcrowded and still deal in paper and antiquated computer systems, you may still see them months and years from the date you file.

Open your wallet, hug your kids, and hold on. You just signed up for one of the worst legal processes we've created. Expect to wait a minimum of six months to even get on the court docket.

Court divorces don't work well. But they work best under the following circumstances:

- Your spouse is fundamentally unable or unwilling to negotiate.
- You believe your spouse is hiding assets.
- Documented abuse is part of your marital history.

Judges don't have the time to consider how unhappy either of you are. Some see more than thirty cases a day, and, to them, this is a business transaction with each side ending up with one thing or another and the other side getting the rest. End of story.

Did you want to tell the judge your story? Good luck. What might you say that they have not already heard and will compel them to wave a wand and judge in your favor? Keep in mind, there are no do-overs. The judge's decisions are final, and you've just invited them to make important financial and parenting decisions for you and your children. And you've just met them.

Turn off whatever legal television shows are playing in your head, and turn your attention to the legal process you are now mired in. It will require your full attention and most of your money.

What's the newest offering from the family law industry? It's called cooperative divorce, and it claims it is client focused. That should tell you most of what you need to know. Every other service offered from the entrenched divorce industry is not client focused. Time (and money) will tell.

The truth is, in divorce there are at least two parties who are in a deep personal transition. Others would be hard pressed to pre-determine that one process or another is better for the divorcing couple. It is up to the two of you. You are the ones responsible for your future lives, and you must choose what you believe is best for you.

Because divorce in America can cost anywhere from a few hundred dollars to over one million dollars, it's a very important decision.

Let's review the primary ways to divorce at this time.

Kitchen table or private divorce: Here you and your spouse make a determination of agreement, sign it, file it, and move on to your new life. Upside: quick, less adversarial, and lower fees. Downside: maybe so quick you missed important details (and there are no do-overs once the paperwork is signed). This way may not include proper examination of assets, income, and equitable strategies.

Collaborative: Each of you hires a specially trained attorney who works to satisfy your interests. The goal is a win for both sides. Collaborative divorces are prohibited from going to court. Upside: potentially lower fees, more respectful process than either mediation or litigation. Downside: if either party threatens to go to court, the collaborative process ends and neither attorney can continue working on the case.

Mediation: A mediator works with both sides towards a solution. The mediator is the only impartial party in this process. Upside: less adversarial litigation, potentially lower fees and litigation. Downside: often still very expensive, long process.

Litigation: This is the process at the end of the line. If you cannot or will not work things out in any of the other divorce processes, you will be heading to court. This is the most adversarial process. Upside: you will be divorced at the end of the court process. Downside: too many to count, including paying the highest fees for the longest time with the most emotional cost. No winners except the attorneys.

Getting an Agreement that is Fair and Equitable

Whether you live in a community property state that divides marital property 50/50 or a common law state that divides things fairly and equitably, the bottom line results should not be materially different. It is hard to overstate the value in a carefully and correctly crafted property settlement agreement.

In the best cases, the parties in fact settle on a written settlement agreement with the full understanding of what it says and does. When a judge signs off on it, request a copy for your files. One tax tip here: your tax marital status is determined by your status as of the end of a calendar year. So if you are still married on December 31 of any given year, you are still married for tax filing purposes. Think about if you need to file separately or whether you trust your soon-to-be-ex-spouse enough to file jointly and therefore save some money.

Retirement Accounts – The Details Matter

Retirement plans should be addressed individually and specifically in a well written property settlement agreement. Do not let your attorney simply and generically refer to "retirement plans." That's an excellent path to an unsatisfactory outcome. In fact these could include everything from a defined contribution plan (typically a 401k, 403b, or 457 plan, where the employee makes the contributions), to a defined benefit plan (typically a pension, where the company makes the contributions), to some combination of these. There are also Roth IRAs, traditional IRAs, and cash balance plans. If you have or are a military spouse, you need to consult a specialist in military divorces so you get the correct amount of the military benefits that are considered marital assets. Let's take a closer look at these retirement plans.

Defined Contribution Plans—You may be most familiar with 401(k) plans, although 403(b) plans are also common— the numbers and letters simply refer to the section of the IRS code that spells out the rules for these plans. In divorce, you need a Qualified Domestic Relations Order (QDRO) to split this account. The account is often split according to the amount of money attributed to the marital assets.

If your spouse had the plan before you married, those dollars will be excluded except for the earnings on those dollars during the time of the marriage. The QDRO is written, submitted, and at some point accepted by the administrator of the plan, which then agrees to assist in the transfer of assets to the receiving spouse (who is not the employee).

Here's an important tip on the transfer of assets in a 401(k) plan: there is a one-time opportunity to take a cash transfer out of the transferring assets to use in any manner you want. Now, a caveat: I do not recommend the use of these funds in any case where it does not fit your overall financial plans or immediate cash needs. Some folks use this opportunity to pay down credit card debt so they start their new life debt free.

If you are under age 59½, you will not be charged the 10 percent early withdrawal penalty when you make use of this kind of transfer. You will, however, need to include any withdrawal in income for the year regardless of your age. All of this must be written into the agreement. Once transferred to an IRA, you will incur a penalty to make a withdrawal before the age of 59 1/2.

One other note on these plans—they are subject to the vagaries of the investment returns for whatever the account is invested in. When you transfer funds out of a 401(k) or 403(b) as a nonemployee, you now have an opportunity to invest it in any way you'd like. Take advantage of that with your financial planner, and make this asset grow for your future.

Defined Benefit Plans—In these plans, employers are generally making the contributions on behalf of the employee. The amount these plans end up with is dependent on years of service, the amount they earn, and the amount the pension plan assets are able to earn. This asset is one of the potentially most lucrative assets in divorce, short of a successful family business. *Do not* underestimate its value.

Professional divorce financial planners use reliable formulas to value this asset. Aside from that, it's a quick calculation to show how much in savings you would need to accumulate to match this monthly retirement benefit. It's a lot of money. Make certain you get your equitable share of this asset.

Again, the *only* way a company defined benefit plan can be divided in divorce is by writing, submitting, and having a QDRO accepted by the plan administrator. No promises substitute for the legally required document.

A QDRO is not used in a defined benefit plan when splitting certain military retirement pay. These plans have their own paperwork and rules that must be strictly adhered to in order to have a successful split and outcome.

Cash Balance Plans—These combine the qualities of a defined contribution and defined benefit plans. But a major difference is that these plans are not invested in the markets. Instead, the employee earns credits for periods of employment. If your marital assets include this plan, please seek professional financial or divorce planning assistance in getting this asset split correctly.

Non-Qualified Plans—Government plans (Thrift Savings Plan, Federal Employees Retirement System, Civil Service Retirement System, and state and local plans) are also divisible by QDROs unless your state has a different specifically outlined way to divide this asset. Sometimes a QDRO is not required to split a nonqualified government plan. When that's the case, again, it's imperative that the plan accept whatever order you expect to submit and that you get confirmation of this prior to your finalizing settlement.

IRAs—No QDRO is required to split these assets. But the split and the particulars must be written into the property settlement agreement. A letter of instruction and copy of the divorce decree are sent to the financial institution holding the accounts, and then the transfers will be completed. Sometimes, you must also complete a form from the institution. In any case, there are no tax consequences to this transfer as long as it is transferred directly to an IRA in your own name. Then it is considered a trustee-to-trustee transfer.

What if your spouse is compensated with supplemental, deferred, or excess benefit plans? Again, a QDRO is not required here.

These plans are rarely divisible regardless of what you may have written in your divorce decree. So a couple of things should be considered here. If this is a material marital asset, there should be a compensating asset given to the nonemployee spouse somewhere else in the settlement.

Another potential solution is to include a written requirement that the employee spouse will send a portion of future payments received. For tax reasons, you may wish to have these payments structured as spousal support.

Some plans do accept a Domestic Relations Order (which is not a QDRO). If the plan you are dealing with is divisible, you must find out and submit appropriate paperwork *before* signing on your settlement.

If you are the employee spouse, you should be aware that payments from these plans are unsecured and not guaranteed. The employee spouse may wish to exclude this asset in negotiations since it is a future asset that potentially may never be received.

While a QDRO can do many things to correctly divide important marital assets, there are some things a QDRO cannot do. It cannot control the value of the accounts. But the agreement can accommodate adjustments for earnings and losses between the time of agreement and the time the

QDRO is accepted by the plan. Neither party should agree to a nonadjustable amount.

We see settlements that fail to specify a precise date of division. This will only lead to future litigation. Make sure your settlement includes a date of division of any retirement assets.

Another important aspect that should always be addressed in writing in the documents that secure benefits to a military retirement plan is the Survivor Benefit Plan (SBP). These can be very valuable and if not addressed correctly, survivorship benefits will not be secured for the non-participant spouse.

In cases where there are several defined contribution or benefit plans, simplicity may be achieved by reviewing the dollar amounts for each spouse and making one transfer to equalize the values and then writing one QDRO to split the plan that is the equalizing account.

Remember, in the best property settlement agreements (always our goal!), the cleanest, most efficient route to equitable distribution is critical.

And costs come from unexpected places. The Department of Labor permits retirement plans to charge fees for processing QDROs, and these fees come directly from the accounts you hope to divide.

The consequences of a QDRO error or omission can be devastating and expensive. Remember, there are no do-overs.

Life Insurance premiums paid to protect alimony

If your agreement states that a spouse is to pay the premiums on a life insurance policy for the other spouse and the policies were purchased after 1984, the paying spouse can deduct the premiums for term or whole life insurance as alimony (assuming all other alimony requirements are met) and the receiving spouse would receive them as income.

Reasons to transfer ownership of a policy include making sure the receiving spouse is responsible for making the payments and therefore has an interest in executing that. It can also transfer the cash value of the life insurance as part of the settlement.

Children, Taxes, and Contingencies—What Payers of Alimony Should Know

Depending on what state you're standing in, supporting your ex-spouse financially after divorce is called; alimony, maintenance, or spousal support. Although it met certain important needs at its creation, over time, it became apparent that if you pay someone for life, they have no chance or incentive to become independent.

Equitable distribution of property ignores whomever property is titled to in the marriage as long as it is of the marriage. Equitable distribution supports the idea that both spouses could be self supportive rather quickly. In actuality, it didn't work out that way so a "standard of living" basis was introduced. We know that supporting two households where there was one before is different so as divorce reform evolves, we've tried everything from formulas to factors to come up with a consistent way to calculate support in addition to property distribution. It still eludes us today.

A poorly crafted settlement agreement can leave the person paying alimony significantly exposed if a child contingency demolishes the ability to claim an alimony deduction. An example is an agreement that says the husband will pay $50,000 a year in spousal support until their child graduates from high school at age eighteen at which time, the spousal support will be reduced to $35,000 a year. Two circumstances for child contingencies can occur that relate to the age of the child and the timing in the payments in the IRS Code. If they do, the alimony gets recharacterized as child support *back to the inception of the agreement*—ouch. In the example above, the contingency that comes into play is the one that says, "The payments are to be reduced not more than six months before or after the date the child will reach 18, 21, or the local age of majority." Since the child in the example will reach age eighteen and the spousal support payments will be reduced in that same time period, the previously paid spousal support will be re-characterized as child support going back to the beginning of the agreement. Since child support is not tax deductible or includable in income, both parties will be re-filing their tax returns for the entire period as well.

It can get more complicated with more children. And there are workarounds that divorce financial planners use to make sure this critical tax trap is avoided. Please do not sign an agreement that includes alimony payments when child support is also involved until you have made certain child contingencies do not apply to your situation.

Other seemingly simple rules around alimony should be reviewed and understood by both spouses so that there is no future re-characterization of spousal support.

What if there's a thriving business to split?

Some ideas to discuss with your Certified Divorce Financial Analyst include agreeing to a stream of payments using 20 year Treasury notes, perhaps a fifteen year payout protected for bankruptcy and the death of either party. Perhaps taking a loan on the business can produce a lump sum of cash to settle a negotiation equitably. The point is to be creative while still striving for the most simplicity possible always considering the tax consequences and timing of any agreement.

Summary

✓ Understand that your divorce is not a game but that the divorce industry has many game like qualities that you need to be aware of before you start 'playing'. It is to your best advantage as a couple splitting up to navigate the way your divorce proceeds together instead of letting the divorce industry move you through it without regard to your history and what you will live with as a settlement.

✓ There are four primary ways to divorce, 1) by yourselves with no professional guidance, 2) with attorneys through mediation or a collaborative process, 3) with attorneys negotiating on behalf of each of you, 4) in court where you give control to a judge you've just met.

✓ We are suggesting a new way – see your divorce financial analyst first, agree on major settlement points including a parenting plan and see an attorney to make sure the legal agreement executes what you have worked out together.

✓ Having the best expertise (as in your attorney hiring the best QDRO shop in town) is critical to getting a settlement you can live with and build on after your divorce.

STORIES FROM THE FILES

No Do-Overs in Divorce
Nuisance Clauses That People Have to Live With

Let me share some cautionary tales about ineffective and poor property settlements I've seen in cases my firm has handled. I've included the material issues that led to a lingering problem post divorce, but for privacy protection of my clients, I've changed their names and identifying details.

Back in 1984, there was a new kind of court order developed in answer to problems that cropped up when divorcing couples split up company retirement plans that fell under the Employee Retirement Income Security Act of 1974 (ERISA). The answer to the complications was a court order called a Qualified Domestic Relations Order (QDRO). The rules for this document are IRS rules, and they allow the company plan administrator to follow the court-ordered division of the plan assets for the participant and their divorcing spouse.

When Sally and Edward got divorced in the late 1980s, their settlement included the mention of a QDRO. The order was never written and therefore never submitted to the plan administrator. Fast-forward twenty years, and Sally, who was to receive benefits, sues Edward for the benefits that would have been received if the QDRO had been written and executed. Since neither was done, Edward, in good faith, made a small cash offer to settle the matter. It was not accepted, and after consulting an attorney to confirm the consequences, a letter was sent Sally who would not now receive any benefits. That letter was never acknowledged and the matter dropped.

This has happened several times. The party who is to receive funds pays for their attorney to write and submit the QDRO, but for whatever reason, it never gets done. Years later, the party goes looking to collect those funds, and the plan has no record of a QDRO being filed. Guess what? You get to litigate some more, and the first stop I'd make is your old attorney's office. You may or may not ultimately receive any benefits. This is another reason to complete the settlement and *all* its paperwork *before* you get divorced!

Here's a spousal support client issue that comes up too frequently. The spouse that owes the spousal support calls to say they can't pay. They ask if the receiving spouse will wait or accept some other asset in exchange. In one case, Julia, the receiving spouse, agreed verbally to accept a small annuity in place of six months alimony (the dollar amounts were similar). She did not seek professional advice before accepting this verbal offer post divorce. Unfortunately, several unintended consequences followed. The annuity is taxable and had a surrender penalty when it is converted to cash, and so it was worth less than the alimony amount. Julia stepped outside the written agreement, so there was no recourse when things went wrong. Finally, of course, when the six months were up, there was still no support being paid.

Recently a divorcing client couple was working diligently to divide their assets. They hired me to help them complete a few details and review their proposed settlements for omissions and errors. Both in their fifties, they are friends but Donna is genuinely worried how she'll fare financially. She hasn't worked in many years, is not computer literate, and wants to buy a town home after the divorce. Her attorney advised her to "take a year off and get her life together."

After I picked myself up off the floor, I suggested we challenge that advice. I can only imagine the attorney believes Donna should be able to live off the settlement for a year while not making big decisions after a transition as jolting as a divorce. Yes, it's true that based on the length of their marriage, Donna may be able to support that position. Although I agree that taking time off from making decisions that can wait is beneficial during a divorce, Donna needs to recognize that she may irreparably hurt her financial position. The husband, Bill, has made a fair, transparent, and generous offer. There are *no* guarantees he will work to sixty-five or continue to earn at the current level. If Bill fails to meet his end of the bargain, Donna's choice is to litigate. In fact, if anything fails in their settlement, her choice is to litigate. The dollars, time wasted, and energy lost will be significant.

But here's the real reason Donna should reconsider that poor advice to take a year off, *even if it can be supported by a system that does not require her to seek employment,* it means she turns a year older without working, she uses up a year's worth of assets that will be difficult if not impossible to replace, and she will have to pay for her own health insurance at a cost of hundreds of dollars a month. Why would any of this be a good thing? Just because she cannot be forced to work for as long as she can avoid it, that doesn't make good financial sense.

At this juncture, I'd like to encourage any spouse considering taking material time off from working during a marriage for any agreed upon reason write up a post-nup and have it signed so that there is no misunderstanding of the expected outcomes financially and otherwise. This would go a long way to overcoming big objections many years down the road when the relationship has changed. It is not negative, it is protective. Now both parties understand their decision to step out of the workforce and that agreement is supported legally. With increasing longevity, any spouse needs to think carefully about the financial impact of a significant time out of the workforce.

A family-owned business that is a material source of income or wealth for the family simply must be professionally valued. Guessing at the value can hurt either party. If you have a business, get it professional valued by a certified business valuation expert. No ifs, ands, or buts. Just do it and include it properly in the marital assets. If you end up in court, this is going to get done more expensively because you've paid time for attorneys and the court in addition to having the valuations done. Save yourself time and money and have it done as part of a fair and equitable settlement.

Common objections to not valuing a business include "it's not for sale", "I couldn't sell it today if I wanted to", "there's really no way to value a business like this", "it's not like we get a lot of cash out of the business, and we pour everything back into it." In a divorce, everything can be valued. Certified valuators are quite capable of assigning a reasonable value to a family business. Every business owner should have a valuation done on their business at some point anyway if for no other reason than succession planning – what happens to the business if something happens to you? What is it worth? Another place we can get a sense of what a business is worth is on the tax return. There we see what was paid in wages, what was deducted for self-employment tax and health care premiums, what was earned in revenue, what was kept in profits.

An example of why valuations are so important to transparent negotiations is Jeff who claimed he only earned $100,000 from his businesses and yet somehow showed business interests on his tax returns exceeding $5M owning three homes and belonging to several expensive clubs. His spouse, Karen, was very concerned about disrupting his businesses since she believed doing so would also hurt his ability to pay her and her three children support. At the end of negotiations, after the companies were correctly valued, Karen received her marital share of the estate which turned out to be over $3M. Had she agreed not to have those businesses valued, her lifestyle would have diminished from a multi-million dollar lifestyle to about $200k/year in income with little to no ability to build wealth for her own retirement unless she decided to scale down dramatically more than her spouse and save the bulk of her support.

I see too many women, but sometimes men too, who are encouraged to agree to a settlement that financially damages the other party unnecessarily. This should never be tolerated— for either party.

Spousal support can be a double edged sword. First, it can keep a spouse from moving on because they are now being paid to effectively stay single. It can also be deceptive in that real life can intervene taking the paying spouses income. The media would have us believe that paying spouses are always lying, hiding, and trying to get out of paying. That is certainly the case for some spouses. More often, there is a real loss of income and the paying spouse goes broke (but even bankruptcy can't alleviate the obligation) and the receiving spouse is deluded into thinking this can never legitimately happen. My advice is to work out a support agreement that is fair but that pays sooner rather than later and is simply a bridge to the future wherever possible and not an anchor that prevents growth and new opportunities.

Summary

- ✓ Bad things happen to good people in divorce. Much of these bad things can be avoided through a fair and transparent negotiation process and a thorough review of your settlement before you sign it.

- ✓ A special note to women or anyone contemplating taking significant time off from the workforce: Calculate the true cost of doing so and make arrangements to mutually understand that cost. People are living much longer and we all will have to renegotiate ideas such as savings, work contributions, retirement, etc.

✓ Before you take your attorney's advice to do something like not work or try to improve yourself financially, step back and reflect on whether that is true and good advice for you or if it is something that historically can be 'sold' to those divorcing. In real life, not taking responsibility for your own well being to the extent that is possible and realistic is a recipe for bitterness and dependence.

PARENTING PLANS

Having a Plan
Living the Plan

Settlements can also be used to manipulate a spouse through parenting issues. Let's look at a parenting issue that was poorly written into the settlement and could have been easily avoided with a cleaner solution. The parents of three very talented children in music (one was already on scholarship in college), pay up to ten thousand dollars a year in music-related expenses. With two more children at home and many years of those continuing expenses, they needed a way to work out how those known bills get paid and by whom. The agreement stated that Dad would pay 60 percent and Mom would pay 40 percent of the expenses. In addition, Mom would submit monthly expenses to Dad, who would then send Mom a check for his portion.

This is an awful proposition for several reasons:

1. Mom and Dad, who didn't want interaction on a monthly basis over finances, would now be forced to navigate this every month for several years.

2. Dad, in the fourth month of the arrangement, was already questioning certain expenses, which left Mom short of funds after paying more than her 40 percent.

3. The children got a monthly show of just how much their music interests impacted the family. What was once a big source of family pride now created negative feelings for all.

A better, simpler solution would be to fund a checking account at a local bank with an initial ten thousand dollars that both Dad and Mom contribute to monthly on a sixty-forty basis. Once a year, they would settle up after Mom paid the incoming bills.

If you have children under the age of majority, it is likely your settlement will include a parenting plan. As with the rest of your settlement, your choices include working it out between the two of you or having a court do it for you. When you let a court decide how you will parent your children, you will have the least control over the outcome. Assuming there is no abuse, do your best to work out a parenting plan with your spouse. Parents know that consistent routines, listening, clear consequences and an absence of criticism of the other parent are the building blocks to an effective parenting plan.

When we create a parenting plan we need to figure out who has physical custody of your children and who has legal custody. Legal custody allows that parent to make decisions about how the children will be educated, if/where they may attend religious services, health issues and more. Physical custody is simply where the children live most of the time. The laws are changing but in general, most courts encourage joint custody where it is possible. Just as in a financial agreement, that may not mean a 50/50 split on time or decisions. It does give structure however to who gets to make decisions. Things can get complicated quickly if you fundamentally wish to raise your children in different ways or would like to move your children out of state.

Parents have creatively come up with just about every arrangement possible when it comes to parenting plans. I would like to see parents take more time to walk through the unintended consequences of their decisions before they sign off on them. One couple Linda and Ellis decided they would live two miles apart and switch their only child's physical custody each and every week between the two homes. This certainly seemed reasonable at first. The proximity would mean they could do it and keep their jobs, Cindy, twelve, would have the most attention from each parent often, and they even decided the family dog would travel with Cindy to each home. As time moved along and everyone moved on with their lives, this schedule proved exhausting both physically and financially. Cindy was constantly leaving homework, clothes, and other necessary items at the last parent's home and as hard as they tried, duplicating each item for both homes became overwhelming. The dog even became ill mannered. Eventually, they realized that in their grief of losing the marriage and perhaps some guilt over the impact on Cindy, they'd created an overly ambitious arrangement that was unsustainable. Cindy's life suddenly revolved around what to remember to take back and forth. They re-visited their plan and decided to switch to weekdays with mom, weekends with dad and alternating holidays. Ellis is a very involved, loving dad but they both realized that parenting post divorce is very different from under one roof.

Parenting Plans were not part of my mom and dad's generation of divorce. The impact was extreme at times for all three of us kids, but I remember it came to a head around the time of college. I was going on work-study, the only way I could afford to go. That meant I carried a full load of classes, worked a campus job 20 hours a week and patched together the rest of the money needed between my mom, my dad, and small scholarships. Well, at one point, my dad decided he didn't want to contribute anymore and I thought I was definitely going home junior year. He came through at the last minute and I got stay but because there was nothing written down and contact with my dad was minimal (and certainly not mandated), I never knew when the other shoe might drop. Today, we can do much better by providing a framework for parents to effectively get their children to adulthood.

Like all good divorce planning, it's best to take the time to walk through many scenarios to see what might make the most sense. It's very difficult to imagine what life will be like as single parents and there are changes that although you may have realized they would come are still jolting when they do. These include the first time your ex dates someone new that meets your child. It can include a promotion out of the area meaning one parent will be physically distant. Remarriage is a possibility. Lifestyle changes – the ones you felt restricted from enjoying while married can impact how well a custody arrangement will work.

Going online and searching for parenting plans brings up a wealth of templates and ideas. If you are unsure of how your parenting plan may work out, this is an opportunity to have an experienced counselor review your plan and share feedback. Typical elements of a parenting plan will include:

Time with each parent

School

Health care

Family celebrations

Religion

Child interest and activities

Discipline and responsibilities

Activities with friends

The property settlement agreement is the contract you will live with and potentially die with post divorce. It is a critical document that if written poorly will serve you poorly after you have divorced. Even if that prospect doesn't haunt you, you'll be surprised and likely ticked off at how much it haunts you as you heal and move into new relationships.

Have you known anyone who is dating a previously married person whose property settlement effectively prevents them from ever retiring, enjoying life, or remarrying themselves? Many, many settlements produce these outcomes. What a shame. You have two adults who have agreed to go their separate ways, yet through poor service they are living with an unbearable settlement whose terms cannot be changed.

I can assure you that the person you were before your divorce is not likely to show up in the divorce. Likewise, the person you become after your divorce may not even recognize that person from before or during the divorce. The point is, when people decide to move forward, we serve them best when we write a settlement that supports them in their new lives to the greatest degree that it is possible.

Divorce is not inevitable when problems crop up in a marriage. But it does happen, and it happens often enough that it impacts the lives of all who are near the two divorcing spouses. Especially their children. Every child of divorce has an individual experience that affects them from the time the first rumblings of separation appear to whatever day they receive counseling or when they decide to move forward from the experience in spite of the many feelings still there. For these children and the parents who love them, I designed a process and a firm that serves to turn the divorce industry on its head. My aim is to move toward more humane treatment of all parties through well written property settlement agreements.

Summary

✓ The collateral damage in a divorce includes our children. Think through carefully what you say and do and agree to in a parenting plan. Your children are the ones who will live with it in addition to you and your ex as you all try to move forward in new ways.

> ✓ Please do not fall into the trap of believing that because your children are young adults, they are handling this transition better than if they were younger. That theory just doesn't hold up in real life. Check in with them, see if they could benefit from talking to a therapist and while they may be insisting they are fine, keep watching for signs that they are not healing and may act out or be stalled in a place of sadness.

WE'RE BETTER THAN THIS

*Why I Started
www.wedlock-divorce.com
Putting the Financial Analysis
Ahead of the Legal Wrangling*

We're better than the way we divorce today, and we can achieve a better outcome. It matters that we improve it because these are real people's real lives, and divorce affects the money they've earned and the children they're raising. Even though they pass my firm's way hopefully just once, we have an opportunity to help them, really help them move forward on solid financial ground and with meaningful parenting solutions.

So how do I, someone who is happily remarried, deal with the depressing subject of divorce on a daily basis?

Well, first, I don't find it depressing. I've been working with folks who are divorced, divorcing, and stuck in bad marriages for over twenty years. It's a working puzzle to find good solutions for both parties, and, in the end, I believe that's the highest goal. Sometimes, people are real jerks and even criminally bad. Most of the time, though, couples are conflicted and could benefit from genuine, independent help that puts their needs first. The family law system in the US does not do this well today. In my view, the family law system is not working on many levels. Family law courts are overcrowded. Attorneys work many different ways including as an adversary on your behalf, as a mediator between cooperative parties, or as a collaborative attorney on a team to assist you.

A consumer issue connected with divorce is trying to figure out which would be best for you. Attorney ratings can be found on **http://www.martindale.com/**. The site gives you basic information. Another way to find an attorney is the same way you find a doctor or dentist – ask your friends who they use. Again, though, your circumstances and resources may be very different from your friend's. I find it very telling that if you do a search for "divorcing without means to pay a lawyer" for example, suddenly all the advice is to simply do it yourself. However, judging from family law attorney websites, the implication is you'd be crazy to divorce without the best representation. What if you're a mother of four children whose husband wants a divorce and you need help getting child and spousal support? What if you're a dad down on his luck and need to modify payments to an ex-spouse and since the issue is not enough money, how will you pay an attorney?

Just getting anyone to call you back can be extremely frustrating.

I started Wedlock-Divorce.com after receiving one too many calls from another ticked-off divorced person. They'd lost most of their net worth and all of their confidence to the family law system that shredded their finances and their family. We seem to have it exactly backwards. Those who want a divorce start in an attorney's office who often suggests a position bargaining adversarial approach and may come around to a collaborative approach but all this is being decided before the client even understands what is at stake financially. When people come to me for divorce planning, it is sometimes the first time in their lives that they begin to understand the characteristics of what they own and how things play out if what they own is sold, kept, or split. There is much to consider and many scenarios in which to consider it and yet, the financial analysis is often done by attorneys who have no professional training in personal finance. When they do hire a finance professional, they hire someone as a neutral party which means they can say what the results of an action are, but from the clients I see, they fail to make clear the long-term impact of those actions.

What needs to change:

Did you know:

- More than one million Americans will divorce this year.
- Baby boomers are divorcing at higher rates than any previous generation.
- In 1960, 72 percent of adults over eighteen were married; in 2010, 51 percent were.
- 100 percent of divorces involve financial settlements.
- In most divorces, you're negotiating two concerns: money and kids.

Why we're proposing something different:

There are many good professionals in the field of family law. What is lacking is consumer knowledge about personal finance so that you understand what you are splitting and its impact on your future well-being. Also lacking is great software to quickly tell you what impact a particular decision will have on your wealth, taxes, and income. We put the financial analysis at the beginning of the process. In divorce we are only negotiating money and parenting issues. That's it.

We start with the last three years' tax returns and ultimately review all your related financial documents. A tax return is a roadmap of a couple's finances. The first two pages are the summary of the schedules behind them.

Schedule A shows what property taxes are paid (and therefore, what property is owned), gambling losses, and more. Schedule B shows interest and dividend income (leading us to the accounts paying either). Schedule C shows the family-owned business and its expenses. Schedule D shows investment sales and purchases so if we needed to, we can see where the cash for those purchases came from. Schedule E shows investment real estate properties.

You get the idea. We learn a lot from the tax return. Because of the penalties involved in lying, tax returns tend to be a closer reflection of the family's finances.

If there is evidence that not all accounts have been transparently identified, we have forensic methods to learn the details of those accounts.

Once we show what there is to negotiate, we A.G.R.E.E.™ to review several scenarios with you on the way to settling over money. A divorce financial analyst reviews your settlement prepared elsewhere for inept financial arrangements and for nuisance clauses that can make it impossible to effectively co-parent.

Then you can return to your attorney to have the documents prepared to reflect what you've agreed to as divorcing spouses.

Attorneys are rarely specifically trained in personal finance and divorce financial planning. They are often trained in divorce negotiation. That's an important difference to your pocketbook. Most are trained to fight, fight, and fight. And those who are trained in more compassionate negotiation are still trained to extend the process as long as possible without ever having to state that inherit conflict of interest.

We strongly encourage you to do something radical and get your complete financial analysis and several scenarios *before* going to see an attorney. Should you ultimately retain an attorney, they can use these reports. Do not go into negotiation without knowing what your full financial picture is.

How it works:

You use the A.G.R.E.E.™ negotiation process to reach a fair and equitable settlement without the tyranny of the entrenched multibillion-dollar legal divorce industry. Financial experts analyze your income and assets today and twenty years from now. They produce work so you can get an acceptable agreement without losing your income, assets, or years to the family law legal system.

Why this works:

All cases settle. If you use the legal system to settle your divorce, this happens when your money is gone. If you use the A.G.R.E.E.™ negotiation process, you keep the time and cost advantage of settling more quickly and less expensively. You still have assets and income at the end of the process. These are critical to rebuilding post divorce.

What we are:

Certified Divorce Financial Analysts are experienced, educated, ethical professionals using a radically less expensive, less time-consuming, more compassionate way to divorce.

What we are not:

We are not a legal mediation firm, or a legal collaborative firm, or advocates of litigating a divorce in any form. We do work with attorneys who also believe the assets you've built together should be split between you and not squandered on a long legal process.

How we can help:

Divorce happens and it doesn't have to destroy lives. We have a better way. We know a better way. Let's be better than our current system.

Use the A.G.R.E.E.™ negotiation process to secure a fair and equitable settlement that gives you both a foundation for moving forward with your lives. The process also addresses settlement issues regarding children.

Accept & Accelerate the process

Get agreement through understanding the financials

Remove emotion by clarifying the financials

Everyone is considered (you, them, kids, pets)

Every dollar counts and every dollar is counted

We apply negotiation science working with both parties. This includes everything from the language we use – we don't challenge numbers, we confirm them (and if they cannot be confirmed, they tend to get changed so they are correct), to working hard to understand each parties highest priorities. This is a rational, smart, equitable way to divide the assets you've built to this point. Many divorcing couples lose their assets to the broken family law litigation system. Don't be one of them.

In divorce financial planning, we have two primary issues to consider: your assets/income and children in the family.

It is tedious and time-consuming to gather the documents necessary to make a financial analysis, and it is absolutely mandatory to the process—slowing this down costs real money.

It's necessary and important to forecast past the date of settlement. In order to understand if we have a fair and equitable settlement, we need to look many years out to see how each party does financially.

Children and pets are considered in the preparation of the property settlement agreement, and if we are thoughtful in our discussions, we can avoid unnecessary clauses that make co-parenting difficult or impossible.

It is truly important to have assets post divorce to rebuild your financial life. The key to having those assets post divorce is to use a real process applying negotiation science so two conflicted parties can work toward a fair and equitable solution that saves you fees and trauma. Position bargaining is simply an ineffective way for two people to get a satisfactory result in a negotiation. One person will, but the other has to basically agree to be financially damaged in position bargaining. Think of it as being a financial bully. Applying negotiation science can seem like common sense and much of it is but it is a more thoughtful way of negotiating in a difficult environment. Everything from speech, language, personal space, tone, length of a session, neutral meeting place and more is considered.

Nearly *everyone* takes a financial hit during a divorce—we believe you can mute that hardship significantly by using this process so that you end up with the financial foundation after your divorce. We do not encourage going back out (for either party) and buying the previous lifestyle. In order to build up financial freedom after divorce, we encourage realistic expectations for the first few years after settlement. Below are typical percentages of income for most basic needs:

Category	Percent of Income
Savings	20%
Housing	25-35%
Utilities	5-10%
Car or Public Transportation	10-15%
Food	10-15%
Medical	5-10%
Entertainment	5-7%
Personal	2-7%
Giving	5-10%

Divorce is disruptive but it does not have to financially decimate a family who has built up assets together—understanding this can help save you money.

Divorce is tough on everyone, including children, so we work very hard to avoid nuisance clauses that are another "cost" of divorce. In this case these clauses are an emotional cost.

You should know that in 2000, the top *three* divorce attorneys in the US firms earned $6.5 million dollars. That was twelve years ago—they earn even more today. At a recent conference, one top paid attorney who appears on television frequently bragged that his highest fee for one case was. $12.5 million dollars. Their pay is based directly on your choices and how you proceed with your divorce. Good for them—it's a market, right? Not exactly. More like a racket and a somehow legal transfer of wealth from your family to theirs. The only winners in a court divorce are the attorneys.

Look, you're good people. You were good people when you married, and you're good people now. Unfortunately, divorce can have even the best people acting and feeling their worst. A job well done by divorce professionals guides you through the process holistically.

We recognize and respect the good work of attorneys who work with divorcing clients in an efficient, compassionate process that helps them reach a positive outcome with lower fees. Unfortunately, this is the rare family law attorney.

Let's take a look at some of the ways the good intentions of the methods above can go quickly awry.

Summary

✓ The foundation of principled negotiation includes understanding shared interests and defining differences between you and your spouse. Standing in the other person's shoes can help make clear what they need out of the negotiation and may even illuminate how you can get there. The same process applies when considering your interests.

✓ We use objective criteria as we move through negotiations: the marital estate value, income, spending, and parenting.

✓ We rely on standards to guide our assessments: appraisals, valuations, statements, and formulas.

BY THE NUMBERS

*Marital Finance
And Divorce Finance*

Good marriages are made of many things, including both parties consciously deciding regularly to participate in and grow the relationship. You will recall that your vows more than likely included a promise to hang out together until death, and with longevity increasing, that's a long ride for most of us.

It matters to consider what makes up a good marriage before we examine how a family gets to the decision of divorce.

It's as simple and as complicated as how we communicate with and support each other. Over many years, this can boil down to blaming the other person, shutting off their opportunities to express how they feel, and using words that indicate all is wrong with them, life, the world.

There is another important piece, and we intuitively know this but often fail to create it. When two people embark on a life together, they neglect to create their own interesting, intertwined life as well. We know that people who develop a full life for themselves (including enjoying friendships, keeping their bodies healthy, staying curious about the world) also share these traits with their partner. Therefore, they bring much more to the marriage than those spouses who would look to their partner to meet each and every need.

Two major advantages come from living life to the fullest inside a marriage: 1) you will actually live a full, interesting life, and 2) if for any reason the marriage does not last, you will have a foundation for living fully going forward.

Economically, it is still true that married adults have enjoyed economic advantages for the last forty years over those who are unmarried. The only time this statistic did not hold up is when the married woman does not have a high school diploma. Those households had incomes lower than their unmarried counterparts. It's also true that if one spouse does not work, marriage does not increase household financial resources.

Before we turn our attention to that other bookend in the family life cycle, the divorce industry, let's briefly talk about a financial foundation inside a healthy marriage. This includes marital financial planning.

Here are some questions to reflect on:

- ✓ What must a marriage offer in order for it to be viewed as a mutual investment in time and money?

- ✓ Do you agree to build something that together you believe will be better, stronger, and more prosperous than if you build it alone or with someone other than your spouse?

The best first step is to take care who you choose for your spouse. If you choose a spouse who is immature in many ways but particularly immature about money, you may be setting up your future for some very rocky times. Picking a spouse who shares your views on money (assuming your views include living below your means and working toward your personal financial goals) is one of the best financial decisions you can make. What if you marry someone who seems delightful and fun but you come to find out they really do not enjoy working, have no interest in working, and never get around to working? That means you're going to be working a *lot*. Think about it—if you are a saver with goals and you marry someone who thinks life is a prepaid party, you're not going to reach your goals and are very likely to be stripped of anything you do manage to build when a divorce eventually comes.

You and your spouse can figure out much of what works best for you on the day-to-day matters of how to hold accounts, where to bank, etc. Foundationally, though, some things are non-negotiable. These include agreeing on who works, who works if there are children, and how to build retirement savings for both spouses, even and especially when the family has agreed that one should step out of the workforce for a period of time. Moving in sync toward a financial future that includes goals you both care about funding and yet allows you both to enjoy some level of independent spending is a good foundation for sharing power when times are good and struggles when life happens. You're truly in it together.

When you get married, you receive an official marriage certificate. When you get divorced, there is almost always a property settlement agreement included with the marital dissolution agreement (different states use different language).

Once in a while, couples will get divorced before they reach a property settlement agreement. This is highly inadvisable. While married, you can assert an action for an equitable distribution for your share of marital property. Should you get divorced before doing this, your rights for equitable distribution are not necessarily preserved.

Because our laws are out of date and out of touch with how families live today, there is a lot of work being done in divorce reform.

There are lots of resources today online, in print, and on television that we employ to understand how divorce is changing. Remember divorce is individual to all fifty states, and in your state it may be changing as well. One resource, the Coalition for Divorce Reform (www.divorcereform.us), covers many topics, including the impact of the cost of divorce to taxpayers, the Parental Divorce Reduction Act, and non-legislation efforts to reduce divorce. It talks about the breakdown of marriage along with the benefits of marriage. While reformists recognize the failure of current divorce laws, perhaps most importantly, they talk about the impact of single parenting.

Another resource that can help you understand what's happening around the country is the Florida Alimony Reform website (www. floridaalimonyreform.com). It details the problems that they had getting divorce reform through their legislature. A recent article advises against getting divorced in Florida because of the state's strong permanent alimony law. The problem in Florida with permanent alimony is that in many cases they get an absurd result. Some pay permanent support who are physically unable to work, and even on their death bed they cannot get legal relief from permanent alimony in the state of Florida. Another absurd result is when a young couple (still able to work and without a lot of assets) divorces after a relatively short marriage and yet one party has been awarded permanent alimony for the rest of their natural life. This is a crazy outcome.

Alimony was put in place to help courts assist the spouse who was not paid for work or did not work for an extended period of time or for some reason needed constant financial assistance. It was not intended as punishment to the spouse who can work for the rest of their natural life. Some of the things that have come out of permanent alimony are antifamily and feel almost anticitizen. They prevent either party from moving forward.

So you have one party who, for whatever reason, is going to have to pay the other party until one or the other parties die. Then the party receiving the support is trapped in their own special hell because they cannot remarry without giving up this assistance. All this sort of paralyzes both people in a position where they cannot move forward with their life. There is something else fundamentally wrong, in my opinion. When two people want to divorce, at some point they should actually become legally divorced from each other financially, emotionally, and in every other way.

A state like Florida makes it nearly impossible to move forward and be separated completely ever again in this lifetime. And part of the problem with Florida's permanent alimony statute is that it relies on trying to maintain a lifestyle that the couple achieved during the marriage. If we've learned anything in twenty years of practice, it's that one of the biggest myths about divorce is everyone will be able to be immediately returned to their previous lifestyle. This is just not the case.

When you take two people and divide their assets and their income into two households, you have additional expense, not less. This is very basic math, and you cannot go out and maintain your previous lifestyle immediately following a divorce. We suggest that you take three to four years to live below your means until you can get your feet back underneath you financially. Then, if it was important to you, you can move on and go after the lifestyle that you had achieved previously.

New Jersey is another state where alimony has reached silliness and in many cases doesn't accomplish what it set out to accomplish. People in New Jersey have gone back to the legislature and tried to correct or modify alimony in permanent status because it does not work as intended.

One well-known example has been in the news about a gentleman who fought hard for alimony reform because he had a lifetime alimony sentence. He believes that the laws have not kept up with the role of women in the workforce. Many of the alimony laws were written in a time when it was common for women to stay in the home for decades. In his case he agrees that there is a place for alimony to be paid to help women or any spouse who has stayed home due to a family request or in some other way harmed themselves economically and now need assistance to catch up economically. He disagrees with lifetime alimony. Some states award lifetime alimony on marriages lasting only ten years. This means someone could be married at age twenty five, divorced at thirty-five and pay until they die at age eighty.

It is possible to sometimes modify alimony after divorce is finalized, but it is very, very difficult and very, very expensive. Furthermore, our family law courts are so overwhelmed with cases they simply cannot consider your individual circumstances carefully, and so they don't. Even when a modification is written into the final settlement, they rarely are achieved and you will have to litigate to make anything happen.

Consider these statistics dealing with the way we live, marry, and divorce. In 1960, only 11 percent of children in the US lived apart from their fathers. By 2010, that share had risen to 27 percent. The share of minor children living apart from their mothers increased only modestly, from 4 percent in 1960 to 8 percent in 2010. *

* http://www.pewsocialtrends.org/2011/06/15/a-tale-of-two-fathers/

A study reported in the *American Law and Economics Review* in 2000, "These Boots Are Made for Walking: Why Most Divorce Filers are Women," showed that the actual parties who file for divorce are women at least two-thirds of the time. The reaction to divorce of some men is never to remarry. Today, just over half of all American adults are married according to analysis of US Census data by the Pew Research Center. And the expectation is that soon fewer than half of American adults will be married. **

And we are waiting longer to marry too. In the past half century, the median age for first marriage has risen by about six years for both sexes, with grooms taking their first plunge at 28.7 years and brides at 26.5 years.**

** http://pewresearch.org/pubs/2147/marriage-newly-weds-record-low

If you're about to walk down the aisle for the first time, beware there's a 50 percent chance the union won't last to your twentieth anniversary, according to a new survey. That number, however, hasn't budged much in the past three decades of data collected as part of the National Survey of Family Growth (NSFG).

If we believe this is true, doesn't marital financial planning make sense? It would make eventual splitting infinitely less painful and mostly already in place.

What's so great about marriage?

Potentially *a lot*. It means your union has legal status. Here are some of the reasons people benefit from being married:

Tax benefits—Married filing joint is a preferred filing status under many scenarios. Estate taxes can be lower for married couples.

Government benefits—Social Security benefits are available to spouses, divorced spouses, and widows.

Veteran and Military benefits—Spouses of deceased veterans are entitled to many benefits, including health care, death pensions, educational assistance, home loan guarantees, vocational training, and bereavement counseling.

Employment benefits—Spouses have insurance options and are entitled to receive retirement benefits of deceased spouses.

What has broken down when a marriage doesn't last? And how can it be that so many people lose more than one marriage in a lifetime?

First, by ignoring what works in a good marriage, you stand a reasonable chance of having yours end. Second and subsequent marriages have ugly statistics that would make you think they rarely work out. Instead, let's look at why some do.

Research on what makes a marriage work shows that people in a good marriage have completed these nine psychological "tasks":

- Separate emotionally from the family you grew up in; not to the point of estrangement, but enough so that your identity is separate from that of your parents and siblings.
- Build togetherness based on a shared intimacy and identity, while at the same time set boundaries to protect each partner's autonomy.

THE GAME OF DIVORCE

- Establish a rich and pleasurable sexual relationship and protect it from the intrusions of the workplace and family obligations.

- For couples with children, embrace the daunting roles of parenthood and absorb the impact of a baby's entrance into the marriage. Learn to continue the work of protecting the privacy of you and your spouse as a couple.

- Confront and master the inevitable crises of life.

- Maintain the strength of the marital bond in the face of adversity. The marriage should be a safe haven in which partners are able to express their differences, anger and conflict.

- Use humor and laughter to keep things in perspective and to avoid boredom and isolation.

- Nurture and comfort each other, satisfying each partner's needs for dependency and offering continuing encouragement and support.

- Keep alive the early romantic, idealized images of falling in love, while facing the sober realities of the changes wrought by time.*'

We've spent a fair amount of ink on what divorce is like today. Why should taxpayers care who gets married or divorced? Because there's a lot of money spent in tax dollars supporting

---

*   Thanks to Judith S. Wallerstein, PhD, coauthor of the book *The Good Marriage: How and Why Love Lasts.*

the associated fallout from divorce. A recent estimate was just under one trillion dollars. That's worth examining.

Divorce is part of a $112 billion dollar cost to society. A study paid for by groups who support government action to strengthen marriages was conducted by Georgia State University economist Ben Scafidi. His study also included the societal cost of out-of-wedlock childbearing.

Some of the costs that are incurred include:

- Divorce team costs
- Lost wages while divorcing costs
- Increased social costs due to divorced families relying on more government support

*http://www.foxnews.com/story/0,2933,351300,00.html

Summary

✓ Divorce settlements mean dividing money and parenting responsibilities. It is not a place to re-live your sadness or anger over this difficult transition.

✓ Alimony is a real help, a bridge to a future for those that need it to get back in the pool of work and independence. It can also be a trap for those who would use it to punish their ex or because they have an entitlement attitude toward their future.

✓ Understanding the limitations of litigation is critical to understanding your settlement and the financial execution of it. There are more than monetary costs to constantly meeting your ex in court. The bills add up very quickly from paying counsel to hundreds of dollars simply to get copies of what each of you said.

✓ There are tangible and monetary benefits to a good marriage. Getting through a divorce safely financially and taking care with your parenting plans can mean a good marriage is a real possibility in your future.

A NEW BEGINNING

The Rest of Your Life
The Rest of Your Financial Life

Here's to your new beginning!

I've heard just about everything when it comes to divorce and its aftereffects. In fact, it's a wonderful opportunity to rebuild a life the way you'd like it to be. There can be much grief involved with a divorce, but there will come a time when you'll know you're far enough into the grief process to be able to move forward. It can sneak up on you even if you're bound and determined to hold a permanent pity party over the loss of the marriage. One day you'll notice that you are noticing others. Every minute, every day is no longer about you, and you welcome that. You may find yourself laughing again, gathering energy, and looking around with newfound curiosity.

Some people seem to never get past their divorce, while others appear to never deal with the causes of their divorce. It would be the rare divorce where both parties didn't play some role in its demise. If you have done the necessary work to understand your role in a marriage that didn't last and you worked out a fair and equitable settlement, you are as well prepared to get back out in the world as you can be.

You know when accepting your role in a failed marriage gets really important? When you're back in a relationship that matters to you and the same things that used to come up start coming up again. It's very easy to let happen. You think you're healed and now understand how to avoid the same patterns as before. In my experience, it takes daily practice to avoid slipping into them. So keep working at being the person you've become through this transition.

Let's focus on you first and then focus on potential future partners. Where you are concerned, we want to pay attention to health, community, and wealth.

Hopefully you've been looking after yourself to the best of your ability through the transition. Post divorce, there's an opportunity to get into the best health of your life. It's the same tried-and-true things that keep us healthy no matter what period of time we're living through with a few extras tossed in. So after you've rested enough, eaten well, and moved to the point of raising your heartbeat, consider adding a soundtrack of songs that are meaningful to you right now.

Healing and Music

There are a lot of moving parts to a new beginning and a new life. One of them, for me, was music. I've been a solid "top 40" girl most of my life. I was not raised in a musical household, although every new exposure I had (including opera in high school) excited me to new ways to enjoy it. In this transition, I changed the soundtrack of my life from an unconscious top 40 to something slightly more dangerous. You'll notice it's a roller coaster of lyrics and tunes. And it really, really felt good. Today, it could included anything from Miranda Lambert but at the time, some of my anthem songs included:

"Stupid Boy"—Keith Urban

"Moving Forward"—Hoobastank

"True Companion"—Marc Cohn

"Love Is the Only Way" and "Thrill of It"—Robert Randolph & The Family Band

"Beyond the Sun"—Shinedown

"Shut Up"—Sprung Monkey

"Right Here"—Staind

"Settlin'" and "Want to"—Sugarland

"Shine"—Anna Nalick

"Nobody Knows"—Billy Squier

"Labor Day"—The Black Eyed Peas

"When the Stars Go Blue"—The Corrs

"Find the Cost of Freedom"—Crosby, Stills, Nash & Young

It's impossible to listen to music and not be moved. Everybody gets to enjoy their own soundtrack, and you might be surprised how different yours sounds before, during, and after a divorce.

I know lots of people who dread dating after a divorce. It can certainly be daunting if the last time you were on a date was in your teens, as was the case for me. Everyone told me I'd meet people through work, or in my travels, or doing things I loved.

Well, that may have happened at some point, but at first it didn't seem to be happening at all.

While many people are comfortable being alone and even prefer it, I am not one of them. I love being in the company of people. Between being a latchkey kid in my youth and a loveless marriage for many years, I've spent enough alone time with just little 'ole me to last a lifetime.

I began to look into online dating. I tried several sites and eventually settled on eHarmony. Part of this was because it seemed to attract people who actually responded with words instead of icons, winks, etc. But it takes a lot of perseverance to stay in a conversation long enough to see if it should or will go anywhere. After a rebound relationship failed and several one-time dates, I was ready to try something, anything else.

And then I met Murray. Online, no less. I'd been dipping into the online pool since a month after my divorce was final. I'd gone through the obligatory rebound relationship and nearly opted out of dating permanently because of it. I had two weeks left on my online dating subscription and, as desperate as this sounds, made that announcement on my profile. It didn't feel desperate at all. It was basically, say hello or get off the proverbial pot. Several did and the one who caught my fancy was Murray. After checking out 1,497 profiles, I'd found my guy.

Going online to date is a bit like shopping, except instead of shoes, it's humans. And it can feel kind of depressing and obsessive all at once. I was tired of it. I needed a break. I'd seen the guys pictured with all their toys—their planes, boats, sports cars, homes—anything that they seemed to think made them a stronger catch. I would put money on the kind of women they attracted. To each his own.

I wanted a real person who possessed certain qualities that I'd decided were basic to enjoying a life together. None of them were based on looks, although I find Murray absolutely adorable. Murray's profile pictures were of him mugging with his adult kids, and one was of him playing a board game on the floor with his granddaughter. The only thing I might have paid more attention to was his profession. He said he was a salesman, and indeed he is a superior one. We fell fast and hard and started a yearlong courtship that involved a lot of phone and travel time between DC and Miami.

Meanwhile, the business plan at the firm in Miami was for me to ultimately be one of two owners in the business. With that in mind, Murray started to look for work in Miami. He has sold technology services to the government for thirty years. His customers are in DC, as is his extended and large family. I was thrilled to learn he would be interviewing locally to see if a move to Miami was possible. In the end, it was not. He would be earning substantially less and, in his case, he owed so much from his own divorce after a twenty-five-year marriage that he could not consider lower offers.

After fifteen months and many conversations, it became clear the owners of the wealth management firm were not truly ready to transition out of the business. I had choices to make. I had been single less than three years. I loved Miami. I loved Murray. Murray was in DC, and I could work anywhere. If I wasn't going to become an owner in this firm, I decided I'd rather trust my fate to my own efforts and start over with a new registered investment advisory firm in DC. So I mentioned to Murray I might consider coming his way. This was a sea change in thinking for me. This was not only never uttered by me previously but I'd been pretty adamant about anyone messing with my future going forward. Moving *again* for a guy? There were many, many moments of terror in wondering if I'd made the right decision.

It was scary contemplating yet another move, another start over, significantly colder weather (my salesman future husband assured me we could play golf most of the winter), and scary taking a chance on someone I'd only known a little over a year.

I did risk it and moved up to northern Virginia in the summer of 2009. We were engaged in April 2010 in one of my favorite places—the Deering Estate near Miami. It is a fabulous property with the most exquisite palms lining a bay that is sometimes filled with manatees. When a full moon is glittering up over that property on a clear night, it is a total commercial for the beauty of Miami. He proposed to me there, and then we celebrated the day back at the Mandarin Oriental hotel, gazing across at the old apartment where we'd spent so many endorphin-filled days and nights.

Married in October 2010, we've settled into a marriage that feels right and like it was always supposed to be. Murray and I have real fights and real times of peace and a whole lot of fun in between. It's a great partnership and a treasured friendship. And a truly intimate dream come true.

So at this point, my story has a happy ending—and I still get those calls from people whose endings have gone wrong. That's why I do the work I do. There is so much more to a full life beyond a great partner and work you love. I meet many people who spend all their time in those two areas. But I also meet many people who squeeze out extra time to help others.

If you are not already spending time in service to others, consider finding a place to do this. Look for something that personally moves *you*, vs. picking something you think you "should" do.

For me, I enjoy things that help kids and veterans and activities that get me outside. The group I found that I want to and do serve is a therapeutic riding group in Loudoun County, Virginia. They help children and young adults who are challenged in many way and veterans who can benefit from the connection with a horse in a therapeutic setting.

What might be out there for you that fits what matters to you? Find it and do it.

I wish you peace, curiosity, and lots and lots of energy. Get back out there! It's a big world and it needs you.

Summary

✓ If you have worked with a competent, ethical, educated Certified Divorce Financial Analyst at the beginning of your divorce negotiations and you used principled negotiation to work out your settlement, you should have a financial foundation on which to build your new life.

✓ We highly recommend you live substantially below your means for 3-4 years after your divorce is final as you re-build.

✓ If the first two items above are true, you should enjoy your new life free of financial worry and ready to embrace an exciting future.

My youngest son, Kevin, with his big dog, Yuban.

My oldest son, Sean, outside his home in Charleston, South Carolina.

A good day with Dad before he left

My mom, Carol Ashby

My dad, Bill Ashby

The view in Miami with morning coffee in my new beginning

My lifelong friend, Karen, whose illness awakened me to changes I needed to make in my own life

At 12,000 feet in Crested Butte taking in the view post divorce

Murray and I on our wedding day.

LOVE-JACKED

Meet the Twisted Sisters: The Wedding Industry and The Divorce Industry

The multi-billion dollar wedding industry:

- 2.5 million weddings annually in the US worth approximately $40 billion to the wedding industry
- 85,000 of these weddings cost more than $100,000 each
- The wedding industry is dominated by small local companies
- Average cost of a wedding is $27,000
- Average guest list is more than 150 people
- Most brides have two bridal showers
- Average cost of photography is over $2100
- 24% of weddings are now destination weddings
- Average age of groom is 30, bride, 29

Sources: Brides.com, TheKnot.com

The multi-billion dollar divorce industry:

- Revenue generated from the divorce industry (including attorneys, therapists, CPAs, investigators and others) has been estimated at $45B to $100B (billion!) dollars
- Social Security benefits are increasingly being factored into settlements as marital property
- The divorce rate among adults ages 50 and older ("gray divorce") doubled between 1990 and 2009.
- Roughly 1 in 4 divorces in 2009 occurred to persons ages 50 and older.
- The rate of divorce was 2.5 times higher for those in remarriages versus first marriages.

Sources: Divorceandfinance.org, CNBC.com, Susan Brown, BGSU: The Gray Divorce Revolution: Rising Divorce among Middle-aged and Older Adults, 1990-2009

Tools & Techniques

Included here are some of the forms we use to organize client files and finances.

Wedlock-Divorce Getting Organized Sheet

These documents should be collected and given to your Certified Divorce Financial Analyst

- ❑ Documents for my CDFA (Certified Divorce Financial Analyst)
- ❑ Documents from my CDFA (Certified Divorce Financial Analyst)
- ❑ Documents for my attorney
- ❑ Documents from my attorney
- ❑ To-Do List(s)

*This information would cover the following:

Personal Information (provided by spouses)

- ✓ Each spouse's name, date of birth, Social Security number
- ✓ Names and birth dates of children, dependents

- ✓ Date and place of marriage and length of residence in present state

- ✓ Information on prior marriages and children

- ✓ Date of separation and grounds for divorce

- ✓ Current occupation of spouses and names/addresses of employers

- ✓ Education and degrees of each spouse

- ✓ Names, addresses, e-mails, and telephone numbers of attorneys

Financial Situation (provided by spouses)

- ✓ Income of each spouse

- ✓ Expenses of each spouse

- ✓ Assets of the spouses (joint and separate)

- ✓ Liabilities of each spouse

- ✓ Employee benefits each spouse receives

- ✓ Life, health, disability insurance policies owned by each spouse

- ✓ Credit reports

Property Settlements (answers determined by spouses working together with their Certified Divorce Financial Analyst)

- ✓ Does a prenuptial agreement exist?

- ✓ Has any married time been spent in a community property state?

- ✓ Have all assets been listed, valued, and classified as joint or separate?

- ✓ Has the tax basis for all assets been determined?

- ✓ If assets will be transferred or sold, have tax consequences been calculated and explained to you?

- ✓ Have loans and other liabilities on the properties (or otherwise) been listed and considered?

- ✓ Is there a family business?

Spousal Support and Child Support (answers determined by spouses and their attorney along with their Certified Financial Divorce Analyst)

- ✓ Have tax consequences of classifying support as alimony or child support been reviewed?

- ✓ Has lump sum support been considered?

✓ Has physical custody of the children been determined?

✓ Have visitation parameters been established for the noncustodial parent?

✓ Has it been decided which parent will get the dependency exemption?

✓ Will spousal support be paid and/or be modifiable?

Marital Home (answers determined by spouses and their Certified Divorce Financial Analyst)

✓ Will home be transferred to either spouse as part of the settlement?

✓ Has amount of outstanding mortgage been calculated?

✓ Will the principal residence be sold to a third party?

✓ If yes, has the tax cost been computed?

Retirement Planning (answers determined by spouses and their attorney along with their Certified Divorce Financial Analyst)

✓ Have retirement plans been listed and interests in retirement plans been reviewed?

✓ Will the divorce decree provide a payout from the plan? If so, will a Qualified Domestic Relations Order (QDRO) be required?

✓ Should beneficiary designations be changed?

✓ Will any IRS penalties apply?

✓ Can retirement money be rolled over to an IRA?

Tax Planning (answers determined by spouses and Certified Divorce Financial Analyst)

✓ If already divorced, was divorce finalized by year end?

✓ If still married at year end, has an agreement to file jointly been made?

✓ Have joint filing risks been reviewed?

✓ Has separate maintenance decree been obtained to permit filing as an unmarried or head of household?

✓ Has head of household test been met?

Documents needed:

✓ All account statements (what we owe, what we own)

✓ Up to three years of tax returns for both parties

✓ Up to three years of business tax returns for both parties

✓ Employee benefit/retirement information

✓ Most recent pay stub statements for a full month for both parties

✓ List of assets

✓ List of debts

✓ Marital property inventory

✓ Non-marital property inventory

✓ Household inventory

✓ Household bills

✓ Credit card statements

✓ Bank account statements

✓ Child support or spousal support (paid or received)

✓ Insurance policies

✓ Any other documents that would have a bearing on your financial situation

He Said/She Said Sheet

In general, the phases below are a summarization of the divorce process.

AGREE Process Sheet

This is the trademarked process that is based on negotiation science so that you and your spouse have the best chance of a fair and equitable settlement. It is the process to use with your Certified Divorce Financial Analyst who will guide you through it.

A New Beginning

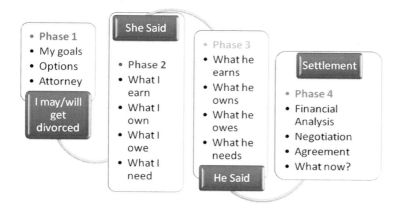

A.G.R.E.E.^{SM}

A—Accept & Accelerate the process

G—Get agreement

R—Remove emotion

E—Everyone is considered (you, them, kids, pets)

E—Every dollar counts

Why this process:

In divorce, parties are fighting over money and kids. In principled negotiation (the methods we use in the process of negotiation), the two parties will either cooperatively achieve an outcome through joint decision making or they will not and become subject to a judge's ruling. Divorce discussions are almost exclusively distributive negotiation—"How do I get more for me"?

Our goal is to use the A.G.R.E.E.™ negotiation process to circumvent the position bargaining legal process by putting the financial negotiations first, then reviewing the property settlement agreement for nuisance clauses that make it difficult or impossible to co-parent or move forward positively.

We know that attorneys will frequently move clients right up to the line of a court date and settle when the money if finally gone. Most divorcing couples who are using attorneys to do their bidding do not appreciate how much control they've lost. The assets they've accumulated will dissipate as fees to their attorneys.

Our process is quicker and less expensive than what the multi-billion-dollar divorce industry promotes as "family law."

The Process:

1. The parties go through the negotiation process with the Certified Financial Planner®/Certified Divorce Financial Analyst™ independently. Here we literally separate the people from the problem (each other).
2. Meet both parties *individually* to value assets (no discussion of who gets what).
3. Have parties independently state what their interests are (vs. taking positions), at the same time acknowledging what they are upset about ("I know you feel that way"), then moving on.
4. Look for trades/concessions that exhibit and promote good intent, and once interests are identified, seek alternative ways to address them.
5. Provide scenario outcomes based on interests and asset values both today and twenty years in the future.
6. Judge the outcomes on objective criteria. ("I am entitled to my former lifestyle" is not objective,

but "These are my expenses and financial commitments" is objective. "You're trying to take all my money" is not objective, but "These are my expenses and financial commitments" is objective.)

Other details:

- We may bring in expert appraisers when a value cannot be determined/agreed on
- People often value an asset higher if they believe the other person will get it. Or they come up with a complex way to get an asset or income to the other party. We often turn this around to imagine letting spouse who puts the lower valuation on it receiving it. This usually ends up in a "re-valuation."
- We sometimes have to take assets into the future because there is not a fair and equitable way to divide it today – these can include illiquid assets such as real estate or an operating business.
- Pension math is transparent with assumptions listed such as lifespan, an earned interest assumption listed and Social Security examined
- Businesses are almost always independently professionally appraised
- Tax impact is transparent with assumptions listed
- Spousal support is considered as lump sum or payment

- Child support is negotiated in light of state guidelines

- Common sense negotiations on other matters that limit interaction post divorce, such as communication scripts and setting up third party accounts to achieve the execution of a settlement. This limits the now divorced couple having to interact frequently over settled monetary issues.

- Once acceptance is acknowledged, the parties can move toward the mutual goal of settlement.

- The process is accelerated by short-circuiting the antagonistic position bargaining usually offered by legal counsel.

- Getting agreement on what the process goals are—settle financially, set up humane co-parenting arrangements, finalize divorce through Property Settlement Agreement effective negotiation (i.e., avoid taking financial arrangements into the future wherever possible). In other words, what can be separated at divorce, should be and what must be carried into the future (possibly due to limited resources or liquidity now) can be done so with effective clauses that do not force couples to constantly deal with their settled divorce as they move forward.

- Moderate emotion—once the parties accept the divorce is going forward and get agreement on the goals of the PSA, we can moderate emotion by fairly valuing assets and income.
- We consider the most important parties to the divorce—him/her, kids, and pets.

Every dollar counts, and we know that cases settle when the money is gone. We work to avoid that result. We do have a clear conflict of interest: if we do our job right, we would like to manage the assets that have been preserved in the process. Every client signs a conflict of interest acknowledgement that they are free to use any firm to manage their assets post divorce. After seeing countless couples lose their net worth to parties they've never loved or who are not parents of their children, we feel strongly we're better than the current system.

Spending Plan

This tracks your monthly spending on the Mine column and gives you an indication of a standard spending amount on the Standard column. You can compare for several reasons – 1) to see if your spending is in line with normal standards, and 2) to see if you are cash flow positive or negative each month.

CASH FLOW WORK SHEET

Monthly Income	Mine	Standard
Wages, salary, tips	$4,200.00	$4,200.00
Cash dividends		
Interest received		
Social Security income		
Profit Sharing		
Rents, royalties		
Alimony	$2,000.00	$2,000.00
Total Monthly Inc.	**$6,200.00**	**$6,200.00**

Fixed Monthly Expenses	Mine	Standard
Rent/Mortgage		$1,550.00
2nd Mortgage		
Alimony		
Car Lease/Pymt # 1		$420.00
Car Lease/Pymt # 2		
Life insurance		
Disability insurance		
Medical insurance		$310.00
Long-term care insurance		
Renter's insurance		
Automobile insurance		
Umbrella liability insurance		
Federal income taxes		
State income taxes		
FICA		
Real estate taxes		
Other taxes/deductions		
Savings (regularly)		$620.00
My 401(k)/403(b)		$310.00
My IRA/Roth IRA		$310.00
My Emergency Fund		$100.00
Total Fixed Exp.	**$0.00**	**$3,620.00**

Variable Monthly Expenses	Mine	Standard
Electricity		$70.00
Gas		$60.00
Telephone - Cell/Land Line		$100.00
Water		$60.00
Cable TV		$150.00
Subscription services		
Furniture/Lge Household		
Garbage Collection		$25.00
Food		$620.00
Dining Out		$100.00
Laundry - Dry Cleaning		
Personal care/Haircuts		
Parking/Tolls		$20.00
Automobile gas & oil -		$200.00
Car Repairs		
Tuition		
Household supplies		
New Clothes		
Season Tickets		
Student Loans		
Entertainment		$310.00
Travel		
Unreimbursed medical and dental expenses		$310.00
Giving/Gifts		$310.00
Total Variable Exp.	**$0.00**	**$2,335.00**

Net Cash Flow	Mine	Standard
Total monthly income	$6,200.00	$6,200.00
Total fixed expenses	$0.00	$3,620.00
Total variable expenses	$0.00	$2,335.00
Discretionary Income (Income - Expenses)	**$6,200.00**	**$245.00**

NOTES: Write exceptions here

Reference:

Category	Percent of Income
Savings	20%
Housing	25-35%
Utilities	5-10%
Car or Public Transportation	10-15%
Food	10-15%
Medical	5-10%
Entertainment	5-7%
Personal	2-7%
Giving	5-10%

Net Worth

This sheet can be filled in to tell you what your net worth is today and what it should be based on your income and age.

Personal Wealth Analysis

Your Name Here
Today's date here

Annual Realized Income			Net Worth Worksheet			
Monthly wages, salary	$4,200	**Property Assets**			**Liabilities**	
Dividends and interest	0	Residence	$400,000		Home mortgage	$300,000
Bonus	0	Vacation home	0		Other mortgage	0
Total monthly Income	$4,200	Furnishings	15,000		Bank loans	0
Other Income (Annual Amounts)		Jewelry and art	2,500		Auto loans	27,000
Business income		Automobiles	30,000		Credit cards	5,000
Capital gains		Other	0		Personal loans	0
Alimony	2,000	**Equity Assets**			Alimony	0
Rents		Real estate	$0		**Total Liabilities**	$332,000
Social Security		Stocks	500			
Other		Bonds	0			
Total other income	$2,000	Mutual funds	15,000			
		Annuities	0			
Total annual realized income	$74,400	Retirement Acct	275,000			
		Cash Reserve Assets			**Summary**	
Net Worth Analysis		Checking account	$300		Total Assets	$748,800
Your Age	56	Savings account	10,000		Total Liabilities	$332,000
Actual Net Worth	$416,800	CDs	0			
Your Net Worth Should Be	$416,640	Money market	500			
Actual as a % of Projected	100%	Other	0			
Realized Income as % of NW	17.9%	**Total Assets**	$748,800		**Net Worth**	$416,800

There is much more divorce math that you should review with your financial divorce expert (who is quite unlikely to be your attorney, unless the attorney is specifically trained in personal divorce finance). This math includes:

What's that pension worth? In many cases it's a very valuable asset. Let's say your spouse expects to receive $6,600 in a monthly pension ($79,200 annually) that he earned while the two of you were married. Do you realize the savings needed to produce that kind of monthly income? Between $1.2 million and $1.3 million in personal savings. Negotiation of pension dollars is critical in divorce math.

It's similar with Social Security (so when/if you re-marry, your prenuptial agreement should cover how you get compensated if you are giving up a good Social Security benefit and the new marriage doesn't last ten years).

Assets—think about it this way: everything you own between you is going to end up in one of three places: 1) you, 2) your ex-spouse, 3) a third party (and you and your spouse will have negotiated how the proceeds are divided).

Anything negotiated for the future (alimony, pensions, etc.) is subject to changing conditions such as death, disability, job loss, inflation, and time value of money. As a practical matter both of you should try to get as much upfront as possible.

The bottom line: everything you end up with is net taxes and professional fees. That's the financial foundation you will build your new life on.

Recommended Reading

Books that might move your thinking forward:

The Comfort Trap: or, What If You're Riding a Dead Horse? by Judith Sills

Tales of a Female Nomad, by Rita Golden Gelman

Design Your Divorce: "What Every Man Should Know About Designing Their Divorce to Have a Financially Secure and Abundant Lifestyle, by Scott D. Martin

Websites that might move your thinking forward:

http://www.divorce360.com/

www.divorcesource.com

http://www.divorcesource.com/ds/idaho/idaho-divorce-laws-673.shtml (if you need/want a quickie divorce in the US, you only need live in Idaho for six weeks before proceeding)

http://www.divorcemag.com/

Made in the USA
Charleston, SC
19 November 2012